Mere Words

Brianna Gaffney

Presentation by *BookLeaf Publishing*

Web: www.bookleafpub.com

E-mail: info@bookleafpub.com

ISBN: 9789357615471

First edition 2022

A Poem Can Be...

Compiled words of Imagery
Unfathomable but concrete
Resurrecting hidden memories

The Comforter

Express to me your happy times
Tickle me with your soft impress
Your sadness rains on my faces,
Blurring every loop, dot, and line
My body welcomes your numerous tattoos

Testimonials
Lamentations
Filibusters
And…

They come in full-force blows; deep scratches
on my faces.
But I do not cry unlike you…
Soaking and smearing the decorative ink
I have to keep my strong binding, for there is no
one else you trust.

You vent. I listen.
Listen in silence, while absorbing every word
you say.
Starting every conversation with the
endearment, "Dear"
Yet you know I can never fully comfort you.

Years go by…
My spine is ragged from your…Confessions
But the cycle begins again: Tickle, scratch,
tickle, scratch.
Soon, I will have no more room.
You'll have to find another comforter.

However, I will always be around.
To remember our time together…
Even after you are gone.

16 pages

I just had to say…
I just wanted to say…
What I need to say…

16 pages,
accounting for diminishing conversation.

47 questions
honest confession,
I never replied.
Did I?
Let me answer you now,
somehow.

47 answers
Feeling the pressure
The urge to explode
The emotions —an overwhelming echo

3,584 words
Many you never heard
From me to you
Confirming what you already knew

Chemistry

First, a glance or smile
Then electricity begins to burn
Atoms going haywire; colliding
Beating, pounding, rushing.

Someone Who Loves Like Me

Someone who loves like me
The one who gives you all you need
Forces you to once again believe
That love is what lets you be free

Someone who loves like me,
May not be seen clearly
I am who has loved you truly
But also recognizes you fully

Someone who loves like me,
Won't be hidden discreetly
You must Love me openly
Or sever yourself from me, promptly

Someone who loves like me
Outspoken albeit Unconditionally
Mindful and Determinedly
Careful yet Stubbornly

Emotional(ly) Bo(u)nd

Scenarios arise in my head
Exhilarating, yet filled with dread
Because I don't know what's going to happen,
Unless said

I'm not your wife
I'm not in your life
Not really…
And it's killing me
Slowly

What am I supposed to say—
Supposed to do?
While I feel this way,
When I'm with you.

You lie
But so do I
By staying silent
I've caused a riot…

In my being
Overwhelmed feelings
Taking on a whole new meaning

And whispering: "Read between the
parentheses."

R.I.P.

I really thought I'd be the stronger one.
I always seemed and was often told,
"You aren't sensitive".
Not like my sister.
But when I watched you stop breathing,
Eyes unblinking,
She and I switched places instantaneously.

Yet one thing I couldn't understand.
How was I able to miss you so much,
And still, be mad about all that happened
between us?
"I'm a horrible daughter."
But surely I can't be the only one, right?

Nothing is inherently fixed but death.
Quite the opposite.
Death forces you to realize what you never did
before.
It's nature's time machine, yet unattainable in
the wake of loss.

Resuscitation

It's just me and you
Discovered me black and blue, nearly dead
You cradled my weary head
I remember something you said, So soft
Enveloped in your arms, Carried aloft
Harshly I gasped then coughed in pain
Hot tears trickled down like rain
But you promised we'd remain together forever
And we'd never part whatsoever
Together we will weather anything new

Writing

It smells like unwritten books.
It tastes like hunger.
It sounds like five or more different voices
intertwined.
It feels like another world.
It looks like blank pages of a notebook.
Writing is all-consuming.

Childhood Memories - Diminish

Mangled Theodore one button for an eye
Take them in again I'm now 88
Better and worse with a mere string of thread

Pawpaw

The original classics are never forgotten.
Old Yeller. The Fox and the Hound. Cújo.
Learned and cherished by a humming
grandfather.

Scary stories. Tomatoes. Sardines.
Rooster calls. Fresh eggs. Climbing a dog house.
Grasshopper catching 'til Nick @ Nite.

Signs & Symbols

All this, and much more, she had endured, but,
in actuality, she was the strongest person he had
ever met, not once breaking her character,
simply theatre talent keeping secrets hidden. He
tried to imagine how it all began with happiness;
her sensing danger all the while questioning if
the danger was all in her head; her mind telling
her to not walk away but instead run; the sudden
confirmation she felt, coming quickly but also
too late, he went even further into his thoughts;
how she felt stripped of her dignity; crying
out—summoning— for a lifeguard.

The Price of Freedom

Inspired by Ed Sheeran's "A Team"

Three years. Struggled to live with it.
Tried to swim, stay afloat
But every now and again
Back to where it began
Weary-eyed, dry throat

Every relapse, more intense than the previous
Been this way since eighteen
No longer occurring only at night
The days she now has to fight
Slowly sinking, wasting

Pull away. Recede the depressing thoughts.
And they scream
The worst things in life come free to us
She overcomes them, thus
Stuck in her daydream

Resignation Letter

It's okay to give up.
Whoever said the opposite is an idiot.
Trust me it's okay to give up.

Give up on things you can't control.
Give up control.

Give up on those that continue to hurt you.
Give up on people.

Give up on finding the one.
Give up on love.

Give up on being patient.
Give up on time.

Honestly, there's no time like the present.
Give it all up today.

Fate of Destiny

It's okay to be afraid, to be scared

But be courageous in the face of that fear
Love yourself. Speak yourself.

Walk your truth
Listen to what calls to you
Follow your deep spirit

For your true soul knows the path that you
should take.
It knows what treasures await you

Take it slow
Whatever happens, happens
Let it flow

Regret: Illegal Affairs

Swore to me
That you'd never regret
But I haven't told you yet
"I'm in love with you."
But I will tell you, Yet
You may regret
Leaving her for me

Defiled: The Aftermath

I know that something isn't right here.
I don't see it but I feel it.
In the shadows
Lin g e r ing.
My subconscious screams,
Yet I am ignorant.
Open my eyes;
Wake—
Wake me—
Wake me up!
Why must I stay?
To relive the same images,
Recurring
 Recurring
  Recurring
   Recurring,
The decline of my ability to escape.
However, this story is unique to me.

The enemy is my own...

Where's My Wardrobe

Haloed by light from the lamp post
I stand in pure beauty
Friendship from an unknown host
Grip the post nervously

I stand in pure beauty
Both awe struck; just aloof
Grip the post nervously
Staring; he at my feet and me at his hoof.

Both awe struck; just aloof
Ask me to accompany him for tea
Staring; he at my feet and me at his hoof.
Surprisingly I nod and agree

Ask me to accompany him for tea
Haloed by light from the lamp post
Surprisingly I nod and agree
Friendship from an unknown host

Malahide

Far away from all others in a dew-covered field.

You only experience freedom here, if you settle.

Bathe in the grand aroma of what you most
desire...your secret kingdom.

www.ingramcontent.com/pod-product-compliance
Lightning Source LLC
La Vergne TN
LVHW050310200726
843509LV00015B/3260